Teaching in Nature's Clas.

Principles of Garden-Based Education

Nathan Kennard Larson

Illustrations by Becky Hiller

Evidence-Based Practice Sections
by Alexandra Wells and Samuel Dennis, Jr.

CULTIVATE HEALTH BOOKS

MADISON

ISBN 978-0-9962642-0-4 (hardback)
ISBN 978-0-9962642-1-1 (paperback)
ISBN 978-0-9962642-2-8 (ebook)

Library of Congress Control Number: 2015906522

Second Edition

Design by Sandhill Studio, Madison, WI

Cultivate Health Books
Madison, WI
www.teachinginnaturesclassroom.org

For inquiries about this book or the Teaching in Nature's Classroom online course, please contact: info@teachinginnaturesclassroom.org

For Sonya Raven and Nikolai Bjorn

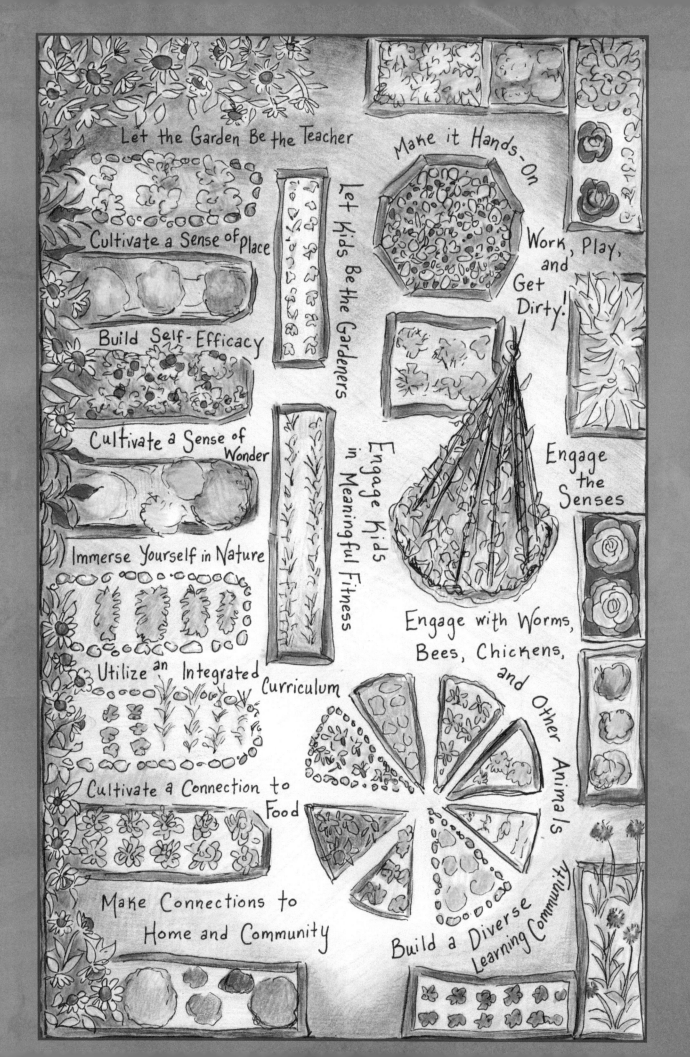

Let the Garden Be the Teacher

Make it Hands-On

Cultivate a Sense of Place

Let Kids Be the Gardeners

Work, Play, and Get Dirty!

Build Self-Efficacy

Cultivate a Sense of Wonder

Engage Kids in Meaningful Fitness

Engage the Senses

Immerse Yourself in Nature

Utilize an Integrated Curriculum

Engage with Worms, Bees, Chickens, and Other Animals

Cultivate a Connection to Food

Make Connections to Home and Community

Build a Diverse Learning Community

Contents

Acknowledgements

I am deeply grateful to the many contributors who helped to bring this project from seed to fruition. Thank you to the many students and educators I have been blessed to work with over the years. I am grateful for all that they have taught me. This book is a result of our time together learning on the land.

I am especially grateful to my friend Becky Hiller for bringing this book to life with her vivid and engaging paintings. Thank you to Alex Wells and Sam Dennis, my friends and colleagues at the Environmental Design Lab, for enriching this publication with the Evidence-Based Practice sections. Thanks also to Alex for her keen editorial contributions. And thanks to Sam for the many years of fruitful collaboration and for his steadfast support of this work at Troy Gardens and beyond. Thank you to Mary Kay Warner for expertly weaving our various threads into another visually stunning publication.

Thank you to my longtime friend and colleague Whitney Cohen for writing the foreword and for her thoughtful review of the book. Thank you to Mary Michaud, Mark Siegel, Carlene Bechen, and Dana Muñoz for contributing wonderful stories from their model school garden programs. I am grateful to Patricia Espedal and Nick Berard for generously contributing photographs. Many thanks to my friends and colleagues from around the country who generously reviewed the book—John Fisher, Lola Bloom, Caitlin Blethen, Erica Curry, Claire Berezowitz, and Emilie Gioia. Thank you to my longtime friend and collaborator Isaac Nadeau for generously contributing his excellent editorial advice. I am grateful to Andrea Dearlove and her colleagues at the Wisconsin Partnership Program for providing such enthusiastic and generous support for this project.

A special word of thanks to my friend and colleague Amy Meinen for inviting me to join her in the development of *Got Veggies* and on so many other worthy projects through the years. She has taught me a great deal about effective visioning, collaboration and leadership. I am also grateful to Amy for her pioneering and visionary pursuit of a statewide youth garden movement in Wisconsin. Thank you to Beth Hanna, Renata Solan, Stefanie Bugasch Scopoline, Erica Krug, Jamie O'Neill, Adriane Morabito, Jenn Sattler, Gerry Slater, Veronica Justen, Amber Daugs and the late Tony Gibson for their work to help move this statewide vision forward through the Wisconsin School Garden Network.

I feel deep gratitude for the Troy Gardens community that has supported the collective vision for robust farm- and garden-based education programming in the Madison area.

I am especially grateful to the children of the Troy Kids' Garden and Goodman Youth Farm— they have taught us a great deal over the years about the invaluable role of a garden in a child's life. Special thanks to Marge Pitts and the late Pat Woicek for their long-standing dedication to the Troy Kids' Garden and Troy Gardens learning community. Thank you to Ginny Hughes, Jennica Skoug, Ida Sobotik, Alisha David, Travus Maloney, Hannah Lavold, Rachel Byington, Kristin Maharg, Elizabeth Gering, Megan Cain, Christie Balch, Jill Jacklitz, Vanessa Ione Machen, Anna Zeide, Casey Bilyeu, Leia Young, Creal Zearing, Jake Hoeksema, Howard Hayes, Keith Pollock, Maury Smith, Marcia Yapp, Michael Carlson and to the many gifted educators and enthusiastic supporters who have helped us grow the Troy Kids' Garden and Goodman Youth Farm into vital learning centers over the years. Thank you to my longtime friends Anthony Hiller, Joman Schachter, and Gene Kenny for their support and enthusiasm for this work through the years. Thank you to Mark Voss for sharing the Growing Minds course with the Troy Gardens learning community. I am deeply grateful to the past participants of the Growing Minds and GROW Institute courses for all of the ideas and stories we have shared and for all of the lessons we have learned together. Thank you to Tom Linfield for his longstanding support of garden-based education programs at Troy Gardens and throughout our community.

Thanks to Ken Swift, Rachel Martin, Nancy Gutknecht, Susie Hobart, Jen Greenwald, Clare Seguin, Dave Ropa, Stephanie Steigerwaldt, Kitty King, Betsy Parker and to the many other visionary educators and community leaders who have inspired me through stories of their efforts to champion garden-based education and outdoor learning at their schools. I am grateful to George Reistad, Donale Richards, Jason Garlynd, Joe Muellenberg, Lesly Scott, Shelly Strom, Julie Jarvis, Ashleigh Ross, Nicole Nelson, Tory Miller, Becky Steinhoff, E.G. Schramka, Robert Pierce, Will Allen, Marcia Caton Campbell, Kevin Niemi, Dolly Ledin, Lisa Johnson, Lisa Jacobson, Mike Maddox, the late Pam Karstens and to the many dedicated friends and colleagues who have worked to create more opportunities for young people to participate in farm- and garden-based education programs throughout our community. Thank you to my wonderful friends and colleagues in the GROW Coalition, GROW Professional Learning Community, and School Garden Support Organization Network for helping me deepen my understanding of the potential of garden-based learning.

I am grateful to Bill Cronon for his guidance during my graduate studies, which helped me build a greater appreciation for the importance of farm- and garden-based education. Thank you to Sandra and Will Dahl for inviting me, early on in my career, to help grow the garden and nature studies program at their remarkable learning center on the farm. A heartfelt thanks to Steve Van Zandt, Mark Nolan, and the SMOE community for introducing me to the magic and power of outdoor education. I am especially grateful to my longtime friends Scott Brinton and Rachael Van Laanen for inviting me into their remarkable learning garden on Coyote Hill. Thanks also to my longtime friends Jeremy Hartje, Mike Einermann, Michael Matthews, Tod Haddow, Alex Jones, and to the many other wonderful members of the SMOE family of naturalists who have helped me grow my skills and passion for outdoor learning over the years.

Thank you to my parents, Margot Kennard and Rick Larson, for instilling in me a love of gardening, nature, and education. Thank you for teaching me about the importance of stewardship and service. And thank you for always believing in me and for supporting me wholeheartedly in my pursuits.

I am so grateful to my wife, Erica Kruger, for all of her support and love. I am inspired daily by her tremendous creativity, insight, and compassion. Thanks also to Erica for gracing this book with her beautiful handwriting. Thank you to our children, Sonya and Nikolai, for their many joyful contributions to this effort. I am grateful for their growing interest in gardening and natural history.

Sure enough, tiny little roots would emerge from the runner and by the end of the season there were even more plants, ready to bloom under the next Strawberry Moon. No person taught us this — the strawberries showed us. Because they had given us a gift, an ongoing relationship opened between us.

— Robin Wall Kimmerer, *Braiding Sweetgrass: Indigenous Wisdom, Scientific Knowledge, and the Teachings of Plants*

No offense to other tomatoes, but these are the best!

— Child at the Troy Kids' Garden, Madison, WI

Foreword

What would happen if every child, everywhere, had access to a vibrant, outdoor space where they could develop a deep, personal connection to the natural world around them? A school garden in which they could harvest and enjoy fruits and vegetables fresh from the source? A beautiful, open-air classroom in which learning came to life? How would these experiences, if woven seamlessly into the fabric of childhood, impact how young people relate to school and learning, to healthy food, and to the world around them?

As illustrated so beautifully throughout this book, a garden can serve as a phenomenal classroom and an outstanding teacher for a child. In a garden we are able to cultivate children's love of learning, their appreciation of healthy food, and their connection to the natural world. With vision, commitment, and some good hard work, educators and families around the globe are ripping up pavement, sowing seeds, and growing garden classrooms because they believe children need to be engaged by hands-on learning in a context that matters to them. They need to know how delicious fresh healthy food can be; and they need to know, right down in their bones, that they are part of a vast and beautiful web of life.

And so, in schoolyards and community spaces across the country, a movement has been born. As a result, new questions have emerged. Chief among them: how do we best use these gardens to achieve our goals and provide all children with the best possible experiences?

In *Teaching in Nature's Classroom*, Nathan Kennard Larson has shared with us a philosophy of teaching in the garden. Rooted in years of experience and supported by research, Nathan has outlined fifteen guiding principles for garden-based educators. Each principle is illustrated by sweet, true stories from his gardens in Wisconsin and supported by evidence-based research. What a welcome resource for the garden-based education movement!

The work of a garden educator can feel frenzied and grounding, often at the same time. Frenzied in that we do the work of farmers, teachers, carpenters, parents, nurses, counselors, musicians, cheerleaders and chefs … sometimes before the morning bell has rung. And grounding in the sense that there is always something that focuses our attention on the present moment. This grounding can be quite literal as we crouch down to pick up an earthworm, tend to a garden bed, mend a drip line, or listen to a kindergartener. With so many beautiful and important opportunities in those first few feet above the soil, it can be difficult to extend our focus up and out to get a big picture view of the field in which we work.

By looking across his years of experience for patterns and best practices, Nathan has provided all of us with a roadmap that can help us select activities purposefully in order to provide cohesive, engaging, and unforgettable garden experiences for the children in our care. These philosophical underpinnings form a foundation that holds up our daily practice, and inspires and directs our work with children. Having worked with school gardens across the country for years, I can say without question that the best practices identified here by Nathan are spot on.

These core principles can provide us with guidance to unlock the phenomenal potential of a garden for children and to keep in mind, as we work with children in our own gardens and in our own communities, the beautiful and vital larger picture of which each of us is a part.

— Whitney Cohen, Education Director, Life Lab

Introduction

I was first introduced to garden-based education while working as a naturalist in the Santa Cruz Mountains of California for the San Mateo County Office of Education. I discovered the garden to be an incredibly dynamic, effective, and enriching educational environment. I had found my calling. In 2000, I returned to my hometown of Madison, Wisconsin, to help build a farm- and garden-based education program on a 26-acre parcel of urban land called Troy Gardens, which had recently been saved from development. Over the past fifteen years—working at Troy Gardens and other school and community youth gardens—I have witnessed the awesome power of garden-based education to touch and transform the lives of thousands of young people and their educators.

Over the years, a number of core principles have emerged for me as best practices in garden-based education. These principles inform sound pedagogy and illustrate why gardens are such essential centers both for learning and for promoting childhood health. The purpose of this book is to present fifteen of these principles. This is not intended to be an exhaustive or comprehensive presentation of such principles but, rather, a contribution to the growing international conversation on best practices in garden-based education. It is my hope that this publication will serve as a resource for educators in the field.

As I have presented these principles in talks and trainings over the past several years, I have learned that the best and most enjoyable way to share them is through representative

pictures and stories from the field. These stories do not serve as mere anecdotes; they demonstrate practice-based evidence. In other words, they help to show that these principles—which have been developed, tested, and refined through years of practice in the field by many garden educators—really work. While the stories, photographs, and illustrations in this book primarily come from the Rooted Troy Kids' Garden and Goodman Youth Farm programs in Madison, Wisconsin, they represent the kinds of marvels that happen daily in school and community youth gardens around the world.

Evidence-based practice

Every summer, I facilitate a weeklong professional development course for educators focused on garden-based learning. The course always brings together an impressive group of professionals. These are schoolteachers, after-school teachers, early care and education professionals, and community educators who regularly go the extra mile to provide their students with something that they truly believe in: garden-based education. All too often, these educators are going against the grain to provide their students with outdoor learning opportunities. Despite their passion and acumen for garden-based education, they regularly face obstacles in trying to get their students out the door.

In the middle of the week, Dr. Samuel Dennis— an international expert on the positive effects of outdoor education—visits the class. He affirms the educational practices and beliefs of the educators by drawing connections to the growing international body of research that supports their work. This conversation often leaves educators feeling inspired, supported, and fired up to get back to their institutions to effect change around learning in gardens and other outdoor classrooms. To continue this productive dialogue between good practice and research, Sam Dennis and his colleague Alex Wells at the Environmental Design Lab have generously collaborated on this publication to demonstrate how each of the fifteen principles presented herein is an evidence-based practice.

Let the Garden Be the Teacher

Some years ago, I was in a raspberry patch with a group of students picking and eating our fill of red, ripe fruits. I noticed a child pluck a large berry from a cane. Before popping it into their mouth, they paused to observe the fruit more closely. They turned it over and studied the underside. Then, they looked back to the spot on the cane from where they had plucked the berry. Then, once again, they studied the hollow center of the fruit. They looked up with a big smile on their face and exclaimed, "Oh, that's why they have holes in them!"

This is one of the multitude of amazing discoveries I have witnessed students make in the garden. The beauty of the garden environment is that in addition to serving as a deeply textured, dynamic classroom for students, it can serve as an engaging *teacher* as well. The garden provides young people with the valuable opportunity to learn through direct observation, exploration, and experimentation. Thus, we optimize the learning power of the garden when our lesson plans and activities support students in exploring and experiencing the garden classroom through their direct experiences.

Teachable moments

One afternoon during a garden session, a juvenile Red-tailed Hawk boldly landed atop a fence post just ten feet away from our garden group. Instantly, everyone was transfixed by this beautiful, powerful raptor. Recognizing the opportunity to observe a wild animal so closely, we quickly shifted away from the lesson we had planned, to engage our students in a facilitated observation and discussion about the hawk. We worked to capture the students' natural curiosity about the hawk and guided them toward a deeper engagement with the spontaneous lesson at hand.

We had engaged our students in a teachable moment. What is a teachable moment? Teachable moments often occur when unpredictable natural events in the garden capture your students' attention. Some teachable moments are dramatic events—like a hawk flying through the garden—and others are more subtle, like a bee collecting nectar from a nearby sunflower, a beetle crawling through the soil, or a just-opened squash blossom. You can help amplify the power of the garden learning environment by capturing and emphasizing teachable moments.

If you are focused on completing a particular lesson you prepared for garden time that day, these types of events may initially feel like a distraction. If this is the case, challenge yourself to incorporate these naturally occurring events into your daily instruction as well as the learning goals you have for your students. By facilitating a meaningful engagement with what is spontaneously occurring in the garden, you will capitalize on the natural curiosity of your students about the world around them. As the veteran naturalist Joseph Cornell articulates, children are likely to remember these moments for years to come.

||||||||||||||||||||||||||||||||||||||||||||||||

" *Nature's spectacles will seize the child in rapt attention…. But even if those special sights are lacking, the child can have an experience of wonder by just watching quiet ordinary things with close attention…. Children seldom forget a direct experience.* "

— Joseph Cornell, *Sharing Nature with Children*

" *I didn't know broccoli grew like that!* "

" *I know why the egg is warm. It's been sitting under the chicken butt!* "

— Children at the Troy Kids' Garden

EVIDENCE-BASED PRACTICE

Letting the garden be the teacher is an evidence-based practice and involves actively looking for teachable moments. Popularized by Havighurst (1953), the idea of the teachable moment has been used by educators ever since. It's now understood that to capture the child's developmental readiness for learning, teachers need to be learners as well, taking the perspective of the child in each teachable moment. This includes the ability to actively listen and to quiet the urge to be an expert. The teacher as learner observes, recognizes and then interacts with the spontaneously occurring enthusiasms of a child, allowing a curriculum to emerge from meaningful child-initiated interactions with their environment (Hyun & Marshall, 2003; Rahm, 2002).

Make it Hands-On

On one occasion, I was working with a crew of students to remove a tree stump from the garden area. It was a relatively small stump, so we imagined that it would be a fairly quick and easy task. As we dug the hole deeper and wider, we were surprised at the extent of the small tree's root system. We ended up needing to dig a very large hole, and eventually, some students were digging from inside of the hole. At one point, a student reached down and grabbed a handful of dense, clayey soil. They emerged from the hole excitedly, holding out their hand for everyone to see, and exclaimed, "Hey, it's clay! How did this get down here?"

Prior to this experience, they had only seen packaged clay in their classroom—they did not know that clay came from the ground. That afternoon, they learned where clay comes from through a direct, hands-on experience in the garden. They experienced a far more profound and lasting learning experience with their own two hands than if they had learned the same information through a textbook or classroom-style lecture. Hands-on learning is an effective method to teach a great range of academic subjects in the garden, from geology to botany to nutrition. This is why a hands-on instructional approach is a cornerstone of garden-based education.

Liberty Hyde Bailey—a prominent leader of the late 19th and early 20th century nature-study movement—expresses wisdom about the natural inclination of children to learn through direct, hands-on experiences in his poem "Child's Realm." The teacher in the poem discovers that, despite the wealth of worldly knowledge he has to offer, the child is most captivated by the living, breathing world at their fingertips. Many children are motivated to learn about the world around them through first-hand experience. Sometimes, the best education we can deliver is accomplished simply by providing our students with the space and support to learn through their own exploration of outdoor learning environments.

At a point in history when students spend more time each day sitting at desks, they sorely need more hands-on learning opportunities in their schooling. The physical nature of the garden learning environment is especially well suited to kinesthetic learning. Children commonly learn by doing in the garden. This approach provides valuable opportunities for kinesthetic learners—who may experience more challenges in the traditional classroom setting—to excel in the living, physical outdoor learning environment of the school garden. Further, research indicates that hands-on learning experiences help children to develop enduring bonds with nature that support an ethic of environmental stewardship and leadership later in life (see the Evidence-Based Practice section below). By emphasizing hands-on, immersive, project-based learning in the garden, you will make the most of your dynamic outdoor learning environment.

A little child sat on the sloping strand
Gazing at the flow and the free,
Thrusting its feet into the golden sand,
Playing with the waves and the sea.

I told how the stars are garnered in space,
How the moon on its course is rolled;
How the earth is hung in its ceaseless place
As it whirls in its orbit old.

The little child paused with its busy hands
And gazed for a moment at me,
Then it dropped again to its golden sands
And played with the waves and the sea.

— Liberty Hyde Bailey,
"Child's Realm" in *Wind and Weather*

"I finally touched a worm. It felt like lotion."
— Child at the Troy Kids' Garden

EVIDENCE-BASED PRACTICE

Hands-on learning is an evidence-based practice. The central role that experience plays in the learning process can be lost in the rush to impart academic skills to children (Kolb, 1984; Roberts, 2011). Hands-on learning in gardens broadly develops a student's capacity for empirical observation and analysis (Kellert, 2002; Mabie & Baker, 1996). In addition, it has been noted as a way to strengthen lifelong environmental stewardship (Chawla 2007, 2009; Davis, 1998). Experiential learning is foundational to garden-based education and recent research has looked at its impact in school gardens (Desmond et al., 2002). A study in Louisiana schools showed an increase in science achievement scores with a hands-on gardening program (Smith & Motsenbocker, 2005). In another study, students in a hands-on garden program had greater nutrition knowledge and were more likely to choose and eat vegetables at lunch (Parmer et al., 2009).

Let Kids Be the Gardeners

At the Goodman Youth Farm, we work hard to ensure that children are engaged in all aspects of the farming process. One season, we encountered a challenge when it came time to harvest the Brussels sprouts. If you have ever harvested them, you know that the stalks are thick and strong, with a tenacious root system that is not easy to pull out. Thus, we presumed that the high school students on the farm would be the ones who could muscle the thick green trunks out of the ground. After several attempts, however, our high school crew determined that

the harvest presented a little too much challenge for their liking. Eventually, we conceded that this might be a job that the adult farm educators would need to take on that season.

The next day, a boisterous group of kindergarten students arrived on the farm and entered the Brussels sprouts, which was essentially a small forest to them. Four children instantly latched on to a stalk and began yanking it this way and that until the roots ripped out of the ground—the plant, children, and all fell to the ground in a tumble of dust and laughter. The children popped right back up and grabbed the next stalk. That season, the youngest children at the farm became the go-to Brussels sprouts harvest team. We learned from this experience to never underestimate the capability and excitement that young people bring to the farm or garden.

The idea of letting kids *be* the gardeners in their school or community youth garden may seem obvious to a seasoned garden educator. Anyone with a background in horticulture, however, can grow quite accustomed to their own style of gardening—including methods, spacing, and planting dates—to optimize crop yield and quality. Furthermore, children who are new to gardening are likely to make mistakes that will affect the garden crops. Thus, sometimes, a strong background in gardening can actually hinder our success as garden educators—at least initially.

Even though we know that education, not crop yield, is the primary goal of a school or community youth garden, we can all struggle, at times, to fully give the garden to our students. By providing children with the space to experiment, make mistakes, and learn from their experiences, we help them to deeply feel that the garden is their own. This is precisely how we cultivate an enduring connection between children and the food that sustains them.

> *We want every [school child] to learn something of why and how plants grow; and the best and surest way to learn is to grow the plants and watch them carefully.*
>
> — Liberty Hyde Bailey, *Cornell Nature-Study Leaflets*

> *I'm gonna' plant this, and then water it, and then it will grow.*

> *I honestly think food tastes better when you dig it up yourself.*
>
> — Children at the Troy Kids' Garden

EVIDENCE-BASED PRACTICE

Letting kids be the gardeners is an evidence-based practice. Children benefit from leading, making mistakes, and interacting with adults who are willing to be learners as well (Hyun & Marshall, 2003; Wake, 2007). Youth gardening and environmental education programs that model scientific inquiry and provide strong opportunities for learning often emphasize direct experience and choice, and support youth as creators rather than consumers of knowledge (James & Bixler, 2008; Rahm, 2002).

Build Self-Efficacy: *Setting Kids Up for Success*

I have such a vivid memory of the student depicted in the illustration above. They stood tall with their clutch of beets raised high, a triumphant expression on their face: Beet Victory! Over the years, I have witnessed many of these thrilling moments—children proudly displaying the fruits of their labors. It is truly inspiring to behold! When children are given the opportunity to plant a seed in the soil and tend that growing plant from seed to harvest, they are truly victorious.

Not only do students gain self-esteem and confidence through their work in the garden, they build mastery. Thus, gardening is an excellent way for students to build self-efficacy. The prominent Stanford psychologist Albert Bandura explains that a "strong sense of efficacy enhances human accomplishment and personal well-being in many ways." Further, he states that the "most effective way of creating a strong sense of efficacy is through mastery experiences. Successes build a robust belief in one's personal efficacy." This is an important benefit of garden-based education because the garden provides many opportunities for young people to experience success. Such successes can be particularly valuable for students who are experiencing challenges in other academic subjects.

Scaffolding

How do we set students up for success in the garden classroom, particularly if they are new to gardening? One effective method is *instructional scaffolding*. Similar to its meaning in construction, scaffolding describes a temporary support structure designed to help students achieve success and greater independence in their learning. In the garden setting, this is an especially effective approach because many of our students will be learning a range of new skills. Through scaffolding, they will master new skills in a way that lets them be active participants and leaders in their own learning process.

So, how do you prepare a planting lesson for students if they have never planted a seed before? One key strategy is to model the activity in such a way that your students can replicate the sowing method and thereby quickly achieve independence in the planting process. For example, you can use a trowel to etch out a furrow row at the appropriate depth for the seeds you will be planting with your students. Then, place three seeds in the furrow row following the recommended spacing guidelines. When your students arrive, they will be able to clearly see and replicate the pattern with minimal verbal instruction. This approach allows students to feel empowered and capable in the planting process even if it is a new experience for them.

There are many good tools and methods available to educators that will help your students feel confident and capable as planters. For example, inserting trowels in the garden bed at the appropriate spacing for seedlings is another great way to help your students quickly achieve independence with minimal verbal instruction. Other helpful scaffolding tools include sowing strings, dibble boards, rulers, tape measures and seed tape.

|||||||||||||||||||||||||||||||||||||||||||||

" *Now I know how to plant, and if I had the shovel and some seeds and soil, I could plant anything!* "

— Child at Goodman Youth Farm

|||||||||||||||||||||||||||||||||||||||||||||

" *It's easy to garden! I'm getting a green thumb!* "

" *You just have to believe in yourself. Then you can make beautiful things.* "

— Children at the Troy Kids' Garden

EVIDENCE-BASED PRACTICE

Building self-efficacy and setting students up for success are evidence-based practices. The concepts of self-efficacy and mastery were pioneered by Stanford psychologist Albert Bandura and have been much studied (Bandura, 1997, 2000; Zimmerman, 2000). Research by Bandura et al., (1996) found that children's beliefs that they could do well in academic subjects depended not just on how well they actually did but also on indirect measures, including confidence that they could manage their learning, peer relationships, and parent participation.

Scaffolding, an idea pioneered by developmental psychologist Lev Vygotsky (Berk & Winsler, 1995), is an intuitive, multi-faceted way to support the development of mastery. Zurek et al., (2014) demonstrated that environmental educators using the scaffolding technique effectively supported children in their understanding of outdoor experiences.

Build Learning Communities

The high school student in the illustration above was a participant in a youth leadership program at Troy Gardens. As part of this program, high school students mentored and taught elementary school students in the garden. It was inspiring to observe how the teens really stepped up to mentor and educate the younger gardeners. I was consistently impressed by the degree of maturity and patience the teens demonstrated when in the presence of younger children. For the younger children, the mentorship of a cool, older role model reinforced the appeal and social importance of the outdoor garden classroom.

In addition to the teen educators, college students and older adults regularly participated as interns and volunteers in the garden. This multi-generational community of teachers and learners made for a robust and enriching mentorship model. Through this experience working with elders, college students, teens and younger children in the garden classroom, I learned just how powerful a learning community can be for everyone involved.

Educational gardens are exceptional environments to support diverse learning communities. They are magnetic, inclusive places that encourage mentorship, volunteerism, and community gatherings. When stewarded properly, a school garden can take on the feel of a thriving outdoor community center— a diverse human community of all ages and backgrounds commingling amidst the flowers and vegetables sharing stories, tips, and food.

Drawing parents, grandparents, and guardians into your garden program is a great way to enhance your learning community. For example, at one of the schools in our area the garden serves as a center and resource for cultural exchange. Parents of different cultural backgrounds regularly harvest and incorporate herbs from the garden into traditional dishes to share with other students in their child's classroom. The school garden can serve as a welcoming entry point for elders in your community to share rich stories and skills with your students.

Faculty members, administrators and other school staff are also important contributors to the development of diverse learning communities centered around school gardens. In recent years, I have had the privilege to work with a professional learning community of teachers focused on garden-based education in our school district representing a range of schools, grade levels, and subjects. These school garden leaders have helped inculcate a culture of garden-based learning in their schools and across the district. One of the outstanding features of the program is a professional development (PD) exchange, in which a cohort of teachers from one school leads a PD session at a different school. On one occasion, a garden-based PD session held on Monday afternoon inspired every teacher in the school to take their students outdoors that week for a lesson that would have otherwise taken place inside the classroom. For the first time, the entire school spontaneously went outside!

||||||||||||||||||||||||||||||||||||||||||||||

❝ *Look what I found! With team effort, we all dug it up!* ❞

— Child at Goodman Youth Farm

||||||||||||||||||||||||||||||||||||||||||||||

❝ *I just want to help people learn about the garden.* ❞

❝ *I love the garden. I wish we could go to school here.* ❞

❝ *Yeah, the garden should be our school!* ❞

— Children at the Troy Kids' Garden

EVIDENCE-BASED PRACTICE

Building learning communities is an evidence-based practice. Numerous studies have shown the value of a learning community that includes diverse cultural, socio-economic, and generational perspectives, including those of teachers, community and family members, teens, and the students themselves (Bouillion & Gomez, 2001; Finn & Checkoway, 1998; Hazzard et al., 2011; Rogoff et al., 1996). A sense of belonging to a school community can often result. In one example, Thorp & Townsend (2001) found that children experienced "comfort, security, belonging, pleasure, and wonder" in the school garden (p. 357). A study on physical activity and nutrition by Smith (2011) that involved teen mentors for younger children found that mentored children had greater positive health outcomes, including body mass index, efficacy, knowledge and attitudes.

Cultivate a Sense of Wonder

Some years ago, there was a student in one of our garden programs who loved to plant. Every day that they visited, they would plant vegetable seedlings throughout the garden. One day in midsummer, they found a remnant tomato seedling in our nursery that was so root bound and stressed from its long stay in a small container that it appeared to be nothing more than a stubby green stick. The child plucked it from its black plastic cell, unaware of its identity, and planted it in a bit of bare soil on the edge of a garden bed.

Several weeks later, to my surprise, the little plant sprouted some new leaves. Right around that time, its mature tomato neighbors were beginning to produce ripe fruit in the adjacent garden bed. One afternoon, I watched the student tending to their little plant when they noticed the new leaf growth emerging along its stem. They paused for a moment to ponder something. They then walked over to the fruiting tomato plants growing nearby and studied their foliage. They walked back to their little plant and studied its leaves once more. Then, looking up in a eureka moment, they proclaimed: "Hey, my plant is a tomato!"

Events such as this continually affirm my belief in the power of garden-based education. What that student learned—driven by their own curiosity and sense of wonder about the world around them—far outpaced any botany lesson I could have delivered in the garden. This is why it is so important to develop a garden program that does not overemphasize the transmission of facts but, instead, capitalizes on the inspirational setting of your outdoor classroom. When we provide children with ample opportunities to learn from their own observations and to develop an excitement and wonder about the garden, we help them to develop the skills and desire to be life-long learners.

As the eminent ecologist and educator Rachel Carson articulates so eloquently, great education is about building relationships as much as it is about teaching facts. Because it is a living and deeply beautiful natural environment, a garden is a rich place for young people to develop relationships with plants and animals. These meaningful relationships lay the foundation for the knowledge our students will gain through their time in the garden and beyond. The garden is an ideal environment to cultivate a sense of wonder. It is a truly magical place—rich, layered, and vivid. Teeming with life and beauty, the garden is a perfect place to stoke the curiosity of a child.

||||||||||||||||||||||||||||||||||||||||||||||||

" *If facts are the seeds that later produce knowledge and wisdom, then the emotions and the impressions of the senses are the fertile soil in which the seeds must grow.... Once the emotions have been aroused—a sense of the beautiful, the excitement of the new and the unknown, a feeling of sympathy, pity, admiration or love—then we wish for knowledge about the object of our emotional response.* "

— Rachel Carson,
The Sense of Wonder

EVIDENCE-BASED PRACTICE

Cultivating a sense of wonder is an evidence-based practice. Rachel Carson's book *The Sense of Wonder* (1956) made a strong case for the importance of wonder and emotional connection to a child's education and later growth as an adult. This was later supported and enhanced by social ecologist Stephen Kellert and others (Dunlap & Kellert, 2012). Davis et al., (2006) incorporated this concept in their evaluation of Forest Schools and other outdoor experiences available to children in the UK and found that a sense of wonder was a shared dimension of positive learning experiences for children.

Engage the Senses

Kids can get pretty excited about the many scents, flavors and other sensory delights to be experienced in the garden. One of our garden educators tells a great story about a student she discovered lurking behind a tall row of flowering fennel plants. She asked them what they were doing, and the child sheepishly replied that they were tasting fronds from the licorice plant (our name for fennel). She told them that was just fine and that they were welcome to snack on the plant as much as they liked. The

child immediately stood up and exclaimed, "Really?!?" Then, reaching their hands into the front pockets of their jeans, they pulled out two enormous clumps of fennel fronds and asked, "Can I have a bag?"

Sensory experiences in the garden create rich memories that can support a lifelong affection for good food and time spent in nature. Michael Pollan illustrates this beautifully in his reflection on time spent in his grandfather's garden as a child: "To lift a bean plant's hood of heart-shaped leaves and discover a clutch of long, slender pods hanging underneath could make me catch my breath. Cradling the globe of a cantaloupe warmed in the sun, or pulling orange spears straight from his sandy soil—these were the keenest of pleasures." By facilitating sensory engagement in the garden for your students, you will offer them rich and lasting experiences that will also help them develop their sensory integration skills. By teaching students to isolate certain senses, you can help them reach a deeper level of engagement with the garden environment. Activities like Joseph Cornell's Sound Map—where students listen attentively and record the sounds they hear around them—enable children to slow down and really focus on what they are hearing. Not only will the students improve their ability to notice a diverse array of sounds, they will learn to identify distinct sounds like the song of a Black-capped Chickadee in a nearby tree.

Sensory experiences in the garden help to foster a deep connection to the natural world. This is especially important today, as children have fewer and fewer opportunities to build experiential relationships with nature. Based on his extensive research, Richard Louv laments, "kids are aware of the global threats to the environment—but their physical contact, their intimacy with nature, is fading." Gardens are incredible places to develop sensory awareness—whether it is the feeling of gritty, sun-warmed soil on your outstretched hands, the sweet aroma of freshly harvested fennel, the graceful beauty of a Red-tailed Hawk circling overhead, the sweet burst of flavor from a Sun Gold tomato just plucked from the vine, or the sound of wind moving through tall grass. It is through these impactful sensory experiences that children will deepen their connection to their garden and to nature and food.

EVIDENCE-BASED PRACTICE

Engaging the senses is an evidence-based practice. We engage with nature directly through the senses, and a number of scholars have stressed the necessity for this connection, particularly during the developmental stages of childhood (Cosco & Moore, 2009; Louv, 2005). Cosco & Moore (2009) have noted the complexity and sensory depth of the natural environment as it relates to children's motor development and sensory integration, and they stress the need for children to have these crucial experiences.

Engage Kids in Meaningful Fitness

When I travel, I try to tour educational gardens and outdoor play environments in the various communities that I'm visiting. Some years ago, I had the privilege of exploring a fantastic nature play area at Boxerwood Nature Center & Woodland Garden in Lexington, Virginia. One feature that caught my eye was a designated digging area! I loved the idea of a formalized place in the garden where kids are always welcome to grab a shovel and dig. One of the first things I did upon my return home was to install a digging area in the Troy Kids' Garden. Over the years, the digging area has moved around the garden—often to an area that we wish to turn into a garden bed the following year. In addition to all of the things children can learn while digging in the dirt, it is fantastic exercise!

Digging is just one of the great ways for kids to be physically active in the garden classroom. The garden provides young people with an excellent place to engage in meaningful fitness. In other words, it provides them a place to be active outdoors—shoveling compost, wrangling chickens, preparing garden beds, climbing fruit trees, carting hay around in wheelbarrows—all in the pursuit of healthful food production. Youth gain fitness as well as a sense of purpose and accomplishment as they grow food for themselves, their families, and their communities.

There are a lot of great tools that can be used to promote fitness in the garden, but there is nothing quite like the ingenious, single-wheel wheelbarrow. This implement provides a very fun and purposeful way to develop coordination and strength while carting loads along garden pathways. Another exceptional form of exercise in the garden is climbing fruit trees. Similar to wheelbarrow work, tree climbing helps young people gain muscle coordination and strength as well as fitness. Tree climbing, of course, necessitates following your program's established safety guidelines to ensure that children are safe and secure when climbing. Once you have your approved safety measures in place, kids will relish the opportunity to ascend into the branches seeking ripe summer or autumn fruit.

The garden is one of those dynamic learning environments where you can exercise your mind and body at the same time. Whether you are walking around measuring the comparative height and weekly growth of sunflowers or digging for arthropods, there are a myriad of great lessons and activities that are experienced through direct physical interaction with the garden. From a public health standpoint, this is particularly important because outside of physical education classes, students have very few opportunities to be physically active during the instructional hours of the school day. The use of the school garden during instructional time helps to shift the balance away from excessive sedentary learning. In addition to providing regular access to physical activity during the school day, the garden exposes students to healthy doses of sunlight, soil, and nutritious food.

||||||||||||||||||||||||||||||||||||||||||||||

" When I shovel real good I get really strong muscles. "

" My hands really hurt from carrying all that water over to the trees. I can't wait to come back and do it again next week! "

" Did you see me? I was walking the wheelbarrow back and forth and now my muscles are sore! "

—Children at the Troy Kids' Garden

EVIDENCE-BASED PRACTICE

Engaging kids in meaningful fitness is an evidence-based practice. A number of studies have shown that time spent in school gardens or 'green' school grounds increases physical activity in children (Dyment & Bell, 2008; Hermann et al., 2006). A recent randomized controlled trial on physical activity in school gardens at low-income elementary schools demonstrated that children receiving outdoor garden-based lessons engaged in significantly increased physical activity and movement over children who received indoor classroom-based lessons (Wells et al., 2014).

Immerse Yourself in Nature

Mulberry season in the Troy Kids' Garden is a euphoric time. The mulberry trees that edge the garden entertain children of all ages as they seek out the sweet summer berries. When children ascend into the trees hunting for mulberries, they enter a deep green world of rough bark and bendy branches, dappled light illuminating the vibrant green canopy of leaves, and juicy, dark purple berries. It is a rich, immersive experience.

Similarly, during the early months of autumn in the Troy Kids' Garden, children begin their time in the garden with a visit to the raspberry patch. They wander

along the aisles, peeking below the spiny leaves searching for sweet red fruit. Although the patch is just about ten feet from the road, I am always struck by how the city recedes from view as children lose themselves amidst the raspberry canes, deeply engaged in the finding and eating of the delicious fruit. In this way, children are treated to an immersive experience in nature despite the fact that they are exploring a relatively small patch of green surrounded by the streets, wires, and buildings of the urban landscape.

How does a small garden in the city facilitate a meaningful connection to nature for a child? Michael Pollan suggests that "although gardening may not at first seem to hold the drama or grandeur of, say, climbing mountains, it is gardening that gives most of us our most direct and intimate experience of nature—of its satisfactions, fragility, and power." Despite the relatively small size of most gardens and the sometimes bustling, urban surroundings, a garden can offer children an immersive and multi-faceted experience in the natural world.

Drawing on environmental preference research, environmental psychologists Rachel and Stephen Kaplan suggest that in regard to extent, "the sense that there might be more to explore than is immediately evident" is "more important than size." So even though an educational garden is far from the scale of a national park, when provided the opportunity to engage deeply in the exploratory spaces of their garden, your students can experience something akin to what they might feel if they were hiking through the heart of Yosemite. Further, the Kaplans explain that gardening enhances "the sense of extent" because it "provides various means of connectedness." Thus, a relatively small learning garden can provide multiple points of connection with its richly layered, exploratory terrain teeming with a diverse abundance of flora and fauna.

Perhaps most importantly, the garden offers children a place where they can feel a connection to nature on a regular basis. It can be a particularly powerful practice for each of your students to choose a specific spot in the garden where they can sit regularly to observe and record the life cycles of various plant and animal species throughout the seasons. Through this type of practice, your students will not only deepen their connections to the garden, they will grow quite knowledgeable about the world around them.

EVIDENCE-BASED PRACTICE

Immersing oneself in nature is an evidence-based practice. Numerous studies have shown the mental, emotional, and physical benefits of time spent in natural environments (Hartig et al., 2014; Frumkin, 2001; Kaplan, 1995). Several studies have shown the restorative health benefits of nature to children in particular, as a buffer of life stress and as a way to restore attention in children with ADHD (Wells & Evans, 2003; Taylor et al., 2001).

Make Connections to Home and Community

Kids have always taken freshly harvested produce from the Troy Kids' Garden home with them, but several years ago, we decided to formalize this experience for student participants. We created a farmers' market stand for kids to "shop" from at the end of their garden time. One day, a child even came to the garden with a small grocery list of vegetables that their grandmother had asked them to bring home for their evening meal. It was satisfying to watch them head home that day with a bag of vegetables they had helped to grow! Children gain a profound feeling of accomplishment when they are given an opportunity to provide for their families.

In our Goodman Youth Farm program, young people are actively involved in growing thousands of pounds of fresh produce every year. We donate the majority of the produce to a local food pantry, which operates within a community center where many of our students participate in summer and after-school youth programs. The students perform the harvesting, post-harvest handling, weighing, packing, and delivery of fresh vegetables to the food pantry. This is a fantastic service learning extension for our students—the ability to grow large quantities of food for the community is extremely empowering.

Another great learning extension is to develop a farmers' market stand program. Similar to donating food to a food pantry, this experience provides young people with an opportunity to grow food for their communities. In this case, students also gain a valuable set of vocational skills related to the marketing and selling of fresh produce in a public setting—as well as excellent opportunities to build their mental arithmetic skills.

The garden itself can serve as a valuable community resource that brings parents and neighbors together. A colleague of mine tells a story about meeting another mother in her child's school garden who had recently moved to Madison from southern India. The mother she met described how she was able to harvest fresh flowers from the school garden for ceremonial purposes. She shared that harvesting flowers from the garden was the first time she had really felt at home in the United States.

There are many ways that the garden can serve as a powerful vehicle for community engagement as well. Invite members of your community to attend a participatory design forum, which will allow a diverse array of voices to be included in the garden design process. Similarly, inviting the entire community to participate in the building of their school or community youth garden will promote community-wide excitement and solidarity around the garden learning environment. Hosting seasonal events to celebrate the achievements of your students is another great way to deepen community connections to the garden. By inviting a broader community to be part of the garden, you will increase the impact and sustainability of your garden program.

> *" Can we make bouquets next week and give them to our parents? Because they deserve it. "*

> *" I'm going to bring my second bag [of apples] to the shelter. "*

> *" Can I take some of these melon seeds home? I guess I should ask my dad though because he might not like it if he's mowing the lawn and there are melons all over. "*

> — Children at the Troy Kids' Garden

EVIDENCE-BASED PRACTICE

Making connections to home and community is an evidence-based practice. Community and family engagement has a positive impact on multiple child outcomes, including social skills, behavior, self-esteem, and academics (Israel et al., 2001). A number of researchers have indicated the connections to the larger community that come from school or community gardening (Armstrong, 2000; Carney et al., 2012). In a review of the effects of school gardening by Blair (2009), all seven qualitative studies reported a strong community-building component that included greater interaction with adults and the community at large.

Engage with Worms, Bees, Chickens and other Animals

Over the years, I have had a good many interactions with children in our chicken run that go something like this: A child holds out their hand to receive a small amount of chicken feed. "Will the chicken peck my hand?" they ask nervously. "She might," I respond. "Will it hurt?" they ask. I reply, "A little, but mostly it will tickle." The child bends down tentatively with their outstretched palm revealing the feed to the hen. The chicken walks toward them, and as she bobs her beak into their hand to peck the grains, the child flinches slightly. Then, they squeal with delight, pop back up with a big, brave smile on their face and say, "Can I have some more feed?!"

Chickens are truly the rock stars of the school or community youth garden. Children yearn to feed them, pet them, and hold them. At the Troy Kids' Garden, one of the most anticipated events is the daily egg lottery, which results in a lucky child getting to take a freshly laid egg home with them. As evidenced in the illustration to the left, children can form some seriously strong emotional bonds with chickens. The truth is that children are fascinated by all animals. Further, in very few structured learning environments are children able to regularly interact with wild and domestic animals as they can in the garden classroom. We often think of the garden as primarily the realm of plants, but by emphasizing the animal kingdom in our garden classrooms we create an infinitely richer learning experience for our students.

The worm is probably the most iconic animal in the garden. Kids love to dig for them in the soil or garden worm bin. They delight in the tickle of a wriggling worm in their hand. Worms also provide an opportunity to learn about the all-important nutrient cycle, which links plants and animals in amazing ways.

Bees are also great animals to engage with in the garden. Several years ago, we began a junior beekeeping program at the Goodman Youth Farm. It has been inspiring to watch young people tend to the hives. One boy in particular gravitated to the hives. At times, he could experience some big emotions and he talked about how the hum of the beehive helped him feel peaceful and relaxed. He liked how working with the bees necessitated a calm and steady demeanor to avoid getting stung.

Children are also intrigued by predator/prey relationships in the garden. Students enjoy exploring these relationships through nature games like Joseph Cornell's Bat & Moth—during which they are able to act as both prey and predator in an active role-playing game. Children also enjoy learning how certain plants, such as fennel or dill, attract beneficial predatory insects like lady beetles to their garden. Even garden pests like Colorado potato beetles excite curiosity. Adventurous students can be given the opportunity to hunt and collect potato beetles from plants in the garden. They can feed them to the resident chickens or, for a truly immersive experience, squish them with their fingers!

|||||||||||||||||||||||||||||||||||||||||

" So the worms make more soil. The more soil, the better the garden. The better the garden, the happier the people and the happier the world! "

— Child at Goodman
Youth Farm

|||||||||||||||||||||||||||||||||||||||||||||

" If I could have only three pets in the world I would have a chicken, a chicken and a chicken. "

" I'll show you the good worm spot. Follow me. "

— Children at the
Troy Kids' Garden

EVIDENCE-BASED PRACTICE

Engaging with animals is an evidence-based practice. Interacting with animals has been shown to lead to greater respect for other living things in addition to having direct positive impacts on mental health and wellbeing (Bratman et al., 2012; Esposito et al., 2011; Frumkin, 2001). In a qualitative study in an urban school district, pre-K through third-grade teachers reported positive changes in children's behavior toward living things and each other during the course of an environmental literacy project that involved time outdoors (Basile & White, 2000).

Work *and* Play in the Garden

A group of children from a neighboring school recreation program once told me that their time in the garden was as fun as going to the pool! We felt deeply honored by this comparison because of all of the places that kids get to visit during the summer, the pool is definitely the gold standard. It was also deeply affirming because we worked hard to make the garden an enjoyable place to spend time. We knew from years of experience that you can achieve all of your learning goals and much more by creating a fun, exploratory learning environment for children.

For many young people, gardens are so fun because you get to do real work. Children thoroughly enjoy the opportunity to use real tools to plant seeds, tend crops, cultivate garden beds, and roll wheelbarrow loads of wood chips and compost. It is fun and satisfying. Further, the garden work serves as a valuable form of developmental play.

Another satisfying aspect of garden play and work is that it gives children license to get dirty! Whether preparing a bed for planting or preparing dishes in the mud kitchen, many young people thoroughly enjoy working and playing with dirt. Furthermore, mounting research tells us that regular exposure to soil is actually quite good for our health (see the Evidence-Based Practice section below).

At the same time, there are also reasons why some kids might feel apprehensive about playing and working in the dirt, from concerns about getting their clothes dirty to fears about touching soil. Consider ways to support your students to help them feel safe and comfortable as they engage with soil in the garden. For example, it can be helpful to have common-use boots, work clothes, hats, and rain jackets on hand so students don't have to worry about getting their shoes or clothing dirty. Providing places to clean up afterward such as handwashing stations will also help students feel at ease about getting dirty in the garden.

Planting is one of the most effective ways to help students feel more comfortable working with soil in the garden. There are few actions as sacred and compelling as placing a seed in the ground. I remember a student who really wanted to plant pole beans around a bean tepee despite their apprehension about touching the soil. As they walked around the tepee with a small handful of beans in their left hand, they leaned their whole upper body away from the furrow row below to afford maximum distance from the soil. Due to their distance from the ground, however, the beans they threw were landing outside of the row. They would quickly bend down, flick the errant bean into the row and shoot back up again. I walked past them several times over the five-minute period during which they were planting the row. Each time I walked past, their body got incrementally closer to the ground, until at last, they were kneeling on the ground and placing each bean carefully into the furrow row.

> *Gardening is hard. But it's fun. It's just more fun than hard!*

> *Sometimes I like getting dirty ... especially when I'm planting.*

> *I'm getting really dirty. That's the best part!*

> — Children at the Troy Kids' Garden

EVIDENCE-BASED PRACTICE

The importance of play and getting dirty are evidence-based practices. The significance and seriousness of play has been validated by research, and several books have been written on the subject (Brown, 2009; Frost et al., 2008; Ginsburg, 2007). Play is considered so essential to child development and well-being that it has been recognized as a human right by the United Nations (1989).

The idea that getting dirty is good for kids found scientific support with Strachan's 1989 'hygiene hypothesis' (Strachan, 2000). Since then, a long list of studies support the idea that soil exposure is good for children, potentially strengthening the immune system, decreasing anxiety and increasing mood, improving learning, lowering risk of cardiovascular disease, and reducing allergies and asthma occurrences later in life (American Society for Microbiology, 2010; Channick, 2010; Lowry et al., 2007; Platts-Mills et al., 2005; Yazdanbakhsh et al., 2002). For an accessible guide on getting dirty, check out the book *Why Dirt is Good: 5 Ways to Make Germs Your Friends* (Ruebush 2009).

Utilize an Integrated Curriculum

At the Troy Kids' Garden we have a much-used and much-loved outdoor music-making area. It includes an A-frame strung with old pots and pans from a local thrift store as well as donated drums and 5-gallon bucket drums. It was originally inspired by the Tree o' Tunes in the Life Lab Garden Classroom in Santa Cruz, California, and over the years it has inspired a number of teachers in our area to install similar features in their school gardens.

One year, there was a group of students who initially were not very interested in gardening, but they did form a strong connection to our music-making area. They spent the majority of their time in the garden creating percussive beats and freestyle raps. As their impromptu music collective evolved, they began performing for their peers on our earthen "living" stage. At one point, they even made flyers for a Friday afternoon concert, which they distributed to all of the students and teachers at school. The connection that these students made to the garden through music was powerful. Over time, this primary connection led them to explore and enjoy the garden through the lens of other disciplines as well. One of the great assets of the garden classroom is that it is so well suited for teaching a breadth of subjects—from music to botany to mathematics to creative writing. Emphasizing an interdisciplinary approach will take full advantage of your dynamic outdoor classroom.

The garden can also serve as an outstanding common resource for teacher collaboration. At one of our area middle schools, the faculty recently engaged their sixth grade students in a coordinated semester-long, cross-curricular learning experience focused on the planning, design, and installation of a new school garden. In science class, students began by viewing aerial site maps of their school grounds to choose six potential sites for the new garden. In teams, the students collected data for each site, including daily hours of direct sunlight, distance from the nearest water source and so forth. The collection of data was carried to their language arts class, where they interpreted it to write formal arguments either for or against each site. After reflecting on each argument, they voted on the optimal site. Once the site was selected, the students developed a list of features for their dream garden.

Next, the list of dream features as well as the selected site and its supporting data were carried to math class. Students used perimeter and area measurements to create a base map on which they could overlay the various design features to scale on graph paper. The final garden map was carried to social studies, where the students developed a formal presentation describing the entire process beginning with the initial collection of data in science class. They delivered their presentation first to their fellow students during the school day, and then they donned ties and dresses for an evening presentation to their entire community, including parents, neighbors, and teachers. At each presentation, they unveiled their garden map and invited feedback on their final design. That spring—after a full semester of collaborative data collection, inventory and analysis, decision-making, design, advocacy and presentation—the sixth-grade class pulled out power drills and shovels and installed their dream garden on the grounds of their school!

> " All the sciences and arts are taught as if they are separate. They are separate only in the classroom. Step out on the campus and they are immediately fused. "
>
> — Aldo Leopold,
> *The Role of Wildlife in a Liberal Education*

> " Nature Study as it comes from the child's enthusiastic endeavor to make a success in the garden furnishes abundance of subject matter for use in the composition, spelling, reading, arithmetic, geography, and history classes. A real bug found eating on the child's cabbage plant in his own little garden will be taken up with a vengeance in the composition class. "
>
> — George Washington Carver, *Nature Study and Gardening for Rural Schools*

EVIDENCE-BASED PRACTICE

Utilizing an integrated curriculum is an evidence-based practice. Integrated curricula and project-based learning are effective ways to teach students and can be aligned with Common Core and other academic standards (Drake, 2012; Drake et al., 2010). In a 2007 study, Krajcik et al. demonstrated that an integrated, project-based curriculum based on national science standards resulted in substantial and meaningful learning gains in students.

Cultivate a Connection to Food

One day in the garden, I ran into a student who was thoroughly enjoying a lettuce wrap creation they had recently made. The broad green leaf was bulging with an odd assortment of freshly harvested garden edibles, including mulberries, fennel fronds and onion chive flowers. I asked them if it was the best thing they had ever eaten, and after pausing to think for a moment, they answered, "no." I asked them what was the best thing they had ever eaten, to which they replied, "Big Mac." "Fair enough," I responded, "I know that is a popular choice. How does it rate up against a Big Mac?" After another reflective pause, they responded, "Equal."

Wow, in the eyes of a 10 year-old urbanite, a spring garden wrap full of fruit and vegetables is equally savory to a Big Mac! As delicious as a lettuce wrap may be, my guess is that in a taste test, most kids would find a Big Mac tastier than a lettuce leaf filled with mulberries, fennel fronds, and chive flowers. So, what made that lettuce wrap so delicious? That child had a closer relationship with that wrap than just about any other food they might encounter. This was a wrap from their garden. It was full of food that they had grown, harvested, and prepared. This is the power of garden-based education. Through relationship, children develop a deep connection to the fresh fruits and vegetables they eat.

In addition to being excellent places to teach young people about a host of academic subjects, gardens are ideal environments to teach children about food. This is fortunate because we live at a time when many children do not know where their food comes from—much less how it is grown. The growing disconnection between people and the origins of their food not only threatens our health but the health of our planet. Garden classrooms offer an exceptional learning environment for children to reconnect with good food and to learn exactly where their food comes from through direct experience.

By teaching young people how to grow their own food, we introduce them to the ultimate local food system as they take on the dual roles of growers and consumers. As children develop an understanding that food comes from living plants, it gives them a new appreciation for the food they eat. A cucumber becomes more than a commodity when linked to the plant that bore it; the rain, soil, air, and sunlight that fed it; and the children and adults who nurtured it from seed to harvest. These types of garden learning opportunities have the power to change for the better the way that young people commonly experience food.

EVIDENCE-BASED PRACTICE

Cultivating a connection to food is an evidence-based practice. Studies linking school gardens to improving students' attitudes, knowledge, and preference for fruits and vegetables, as well as increasing consumption of those fruits and vegetables, are numerous (for some examples, see Gatto et al., 2012; McAleese & Rankin, 2007; Ratcliffe et al., 2011). In one study of 43 children, Hermann et al., (2006) found that the number of children reporting that they ate vegetables every day increased from 21% to 44% after participation in an after-school education and gardening program. In another, a pre/post-survey of 83 parents found a significant increase in the frequency their grade-school child asked for fruits or vegetables at home after participating in a YMCA summer camp gardening program (Heim et al., 2011).

Cultivate a Sense of Place

You know that your garden program is accomplishing something extraordinary and lasting when you begin to overhear your students saying things like, "I love this place, it brings back good memories" or "I wish we could stay here all day" or "If I won $100,000, I would donate it to this place!" These quotes from children at the Troy Kids' Garden illustrate how young people can form extremely strong connections to important places in their lives. When we provide our students with an outdoor learning environment to which they feel deeply connected, a remarkable learning process can unfold.

Cultivating a sense of place is a key—and sometimes underestimated—component of a successful garden-based education program. As educators, we can become so preoccupied by lesson plans, planned activities and other programming that we lose sight of the essential relationship to be cultivated between our students and the garden itself. The emotional bond that young people form with the garden and the garden community will provide fertile ground for deep learning and connection. If you can help your students feel that the garden is their garden, their place, your program will truly thrive. As empowered caretakers of the garden, children gain a sense of place as well as a sense of purpose as they grow food throughout the season.

In *The Geography of Childhood*, Gary Paul Nabhan and Stephen Trimble express a sincere concern "about how few children now grow up incorporating plants, animals, and places into their sense of home." This is concerning—children need these types of connections. I am always struck by how children speak about wanting to live in the garden. As young people form bonds with their garden, as the plants and trees and rocks and animals that live there become familiar and comforting, it does begin to evoke a sense of home. Students can benefit from these types of connections in their lives, and from these special outdoor places in their neighborhoods and communities.

In the school or community youth garden, a sense of place is cultivated in community—a diverse human community of children and adults engaged in the co-creation of an educational garden. Together, they create an enriching learning environment that is embedded in the fabric of the neighborhood. It is a place for children to connect to nature and good food. It is a place for children to learn about the world. It is a place of rich experiences, memories and dreams.

EVIDENCE-BASED PRACTICE

Cultivating a sense of place is an evidence-based practice. Numerous studies have shown that a sense of place contributes to well-being, health and community in children and adults and has biological correlates in the human brain (Lengen & Kistemann, 2012; Derr, 2002; Sobel, 1998; Gesler, 1992). A study of children in Canberra, Australia, by Measham (2007) found that experiential place-based education in childhood strongly influenced family engagement, understanding of environmental issues, and environmental stewardship.

epilogue: Growing Hope

In 2008, I attended the Slow Food Terra Madre global gathering of food communities in Turin, Italy. Our Troy Farm and Gardens team joined more than 6,000 delegates from over 130 countries around the world to network, learn together, and grow the good food movement. At the opening ceremony—held in a large arena originally built for the 2006 winter Olympics—we were uplifted by music, celebration, and speeches by luminaries such as Vandana Shiva, Alice Waters, and Carlo Petrini. Then a young man named Sam Levin took the stage. He was a 15- year-old high school student from Massachusetts, and he told us a story about a school garden project he had started with some of his fellow students called Project Sprout. At the conclusion of his speech, the entire stadium erupted in ecstatic, thundering applause. He brought the house down.

Afterwards I wondered what had made his speech so resonant and powerful. Why did it make such a strong impression on this distinguished international assemblage of farmers, food producers, chefs, educators, students, and food activists? He told a good story, that was certain. It was something deeper and more enduring though, I think, that stirred the crowd so profoundly that evening. Sam Levin had offered us the gift of hope. In his closing remarks, he looked at us and said, "What all of you have started is an unbelievable beginning to a powerful revolution. But I know that all of you are wondering if my generation will be able to continue that revolution and take it to the extent of its mission. Well, I'm here today because I want you to know that we got it!"

A story about a dedicated group of young people growing a thriving garden program at their school certainly fills people with hope. This is another significant gift that school and youth gardens give us. These are places where we can grow hope—students, educators, families—all of us, together. And children need hope right now. Young people are presently facing a formidable slew of global environmental problems that will continue into the foreseeable future. It's important that children have access to places like gardens where they can feel joy and connection in nature, as opposed to guilt and sorrow about manifold problems that are mostly—or completely— out of their control, such as melting glaciers and deforestation. In this regard, David Sobel rightly claims that children should "have an opportunity to bond with the natural world, to learn to love it and feel comfortable in it, before being asked to heal its wounds."

At the same time, gardens provide more than nearby places where young people can connect to nature on a regular basis. The growing of hope is not a solely ideological activity in a garden. Gardens are also places of direct action—lived and experienced from seed to table to soil. On this point, Ron Finley asserts that "planting a garden has the power to change the world and even you can do it." In a video about Climate Victory Gardens, he elaborates in explaining that "regenerative gardening actually helps reverse climate change by building soil. It's like magic!"

The suggestion that a small action like employing regenerative gardening methods in your school, home, or community garden can make a difference in addressing a major global crisis is a powerful idea. It is the kind of idea that can germinate to give young people, and all of us, a reason for hope— and serve as a catalyst for further action propelled by that hope.

Through our work supporting garden classrooms, we can help to provide young people with places where they can bond with nature, grow hope, and take action for the planet. Wangari Maathai sagely teaches us that "education, if it means anything, should not take people away from the land, but instill in them even more respect for it....The future of the planet concerns all of us, and all of us should do what we can to protect it." This is precious guidance for all of us and it should be heeded. During his Terra Madre speech, Sam Levin proclaimed "there are kids all over the world who want to make this happen. All they need is a little hope and inspiration." Now is the time to grow that hope, together in the garden, because our future depends on it.

||||||||||||||||||||||||||||||||||||||||||||||||||

" I like coming to Troy Gardens because it's beautiful and it makes me feel good and excited. "

" Troy Gardens means a lot to me because we have to be responsible and take care of our plants and make sure they don't die. "

— Children at the Troy Kids' Garden

A Note on Collecting Evidence

From the desk of the Environmental Design Lab

Dear practitioner,

While those of us in the world of garden-based education see its positive impacts every day, youth garden champions often face the task of convincing administrators and funders of its worth. Evidence for the beneficial impacts of youth gardening comes in many forms, and you can collect this evidence yourself.

First, ask yourself and your colleagues and partners what kinds of things potential supporters would like to know. You can collect evidence on exposure or use, family or community engagement, long-term stewardship, physical activity, or healthy eating, just to name a few. After you've thought about the kinds of topics you'd like more information on, assess your time and resources. Who is available to help? Can you find volunteers or someone who would like to take the lead on an interesting project?

With answers to these questions, you'll be well on your way to collecting your own evidence for the positive impacts of youth gardening. See the next page for some research and evaluation ideas and techniques.

Here are some ways you can collect your own evidence:

1 **Collect count data on your garden use.** For example, you can document how many kids use the garden, and for how long (e.g., hours per week, per class, or per season). You can count volunteer hours, family participation, or return visits. To assess family engagement, you might ask how many children came in with family members, and how long they stayed. How many children have returned each year? Educators or program staff can often collect this data fairly easily by filling out a form or notebook at the end of each garden visit and by asking visitors a few questions.

2 **Collect data on a particular topic.** For example, you may want to know how youth gardening impacts nutrition behaviors in kids. You can observe children in the garden tasting garden produce. You can ask children about their willingness to try new fruits or vegetables. You can ask parents and caregivers about their children's eating habits. Collecting topical data before and after a gardening program is one way to see potential changes.

3 **Conduct surveys, interviews, or focus groups.** Each of these methods has its own advantages and challenges, but all offer good ways to get more information from educators, parents and caregivers, community members, and children. Online and paper surveys are good ways to collect simpler data, while interviews and focus groups allow you to go in depth with particular topics. Children can even conduct surveys themselves.

4 **Conduct a study.** There is a pressing need for more studies that show the positive impacts of garden-based education. The published studies cited in this book often came about through partnerships between educators, youth garden organizations, and academic researchers. Researchers can provide valuable expertise on research design and evaluation, and studies often come with funding opportunities to offset the extra costs of participation and staff time. Inquire at your local college or university for interested partners, or ask parents and caregivers, community members or other staff members who they might know or recommend. Starting a conversation with a researcher can lead to a fruitful long-term partnership.

References

Epigraph

Kimmerer, R. W. (2013). *Braiding sweetgrass: Indigenous wisdom, scientific knowledge, and the teachings of plants* (p. 25). Minneapolis, MN: Milkweed Editions.

Let the Garden Be the Teacher

Cornell, J. (1998). *Sharing nature with children* (pp. 14-15). Nevada City, CA: DAWN Publications.

Havighurst, R. J. (1953). *Human development and education*. New York, NY: D. McKay.

Havighurst first popularized the term "teachable moment."

Hyun, E., & Marshall, J. D. (2003). Teachable moment-oriented curriculum practice in early childhood education. *Journal of Curriculum Studies, 35*(1), 111-127.

Hyun and Marshall offer a critique that education is not just about teaching—teachers need to be learners as well, letting the child take the lead.

Rahm, J. (2002). Emergent learning opportunities in an inner-city youth gardening program. *Journal of Research in Science Teaching, 39*(2), 164-184.

In an informal, experiential youth gardening program, a learning community emerged from the garden environment through students' engagement in activities they deemed valuable, meaningful and authentic.

Make it Hands-On

Bailey, L. H. (1919). Child's realm. *Wind and weather* (p. 119). Ithaca, NY: The Comstock Publishing Company.

Chawla, L. (2007). Childhood experiences associated with care for the natural world: A theoretical framework for empirical results. *Children Youth and Environments, 17*(4), 144-170.

Adult environmental stewardship is associated with positive nature experiences and role models in childhood.

Chawla, L. (2009). Growing up green: Becoming an agent of care for the natural world. *The Journal of Developmental Processes, 4*(1), 6-23.

Chawla examines developmental paths to active care for the natural world in childhood, and how children develop empathy and sympathy for other living things.

Davis, J. (1998). Young children, environmental education, and the future. *Early Childhood Education Journal, 26*(2), 117-123.

Davis discusses environmental education advocacy and the challenges that educators must address to give children the tools to create a sustainable future.

Desmond, D., Grieshop, J., & Subramaniam, A. (2002). Revisiting garden based learning in basic education: Philosophical roots, historical foundations, best practices and products, impacts, outcomes, and future directions. *International Institute for Educational Planning*.

Grieshop and Subramaniam give an international perspective and thorough overview of the educational theory, history, and best practices of garden-based education.

Kellert, S. R. (2002). Experiencing nature: Affective, cognitive, and evaluative development in children. In P. H. Kahn & S. R. Kellert (Eds.), *Children and nature: Psychological, sociocultural, and evolutionary investigations* (pp. 117-151). Cambridge, MA: MIT Press.

Contact with nature has a positive effect on various aspects of children's maturation, including emotional, cognitive, and values-related development.

Kolb, D. A. (1984). *Experiential learning: Experience as the source of learning and development*. Englewood Cliffs, NJ: Prentice-Hall.

Mabie, R., & Baker, M. (1996). A comparison of experiential instructional strategies upon the science process skills of urban elementary students. *Journal of Agricultural Education, 37*, 1-7.

Participation in agriculturally-oriented experiential learning positively impacts the development of science skills.

Parmer, S. M., Salisbury-Glennon, J., Shannon, D., & Struempler, B. (2009). School gardens: An experiential learning approach for a nutrition education program to increase fruit and vegetable knowledge, preference, and consumption among second-grade students. *Journal of Nutrition Education and Behavior, 41*(3), 212-217.

Experiential learning in a school garden leads to increases in fruit and vegetable consumption.

Rahm, J. (2002). Emergent learning opportunities in an inner-city youth gardening program. *Journal of Research in Science Teaching, 39*(2), 164-184.

In an informal, experiential youth gardening program, a learning community emerged from the garden environment through students' engagement in activities they deemed valuable, meaningful and authentic.

Roberts, J. W. (2011). *Beyond learning by doing: Theoretical currents in experiential education.* Florence, KY: Routledge, Taylor & Francis Group.

Smith, L. L., & Motsenbocker, C. E. (2005). Impact of hands-on science through school gardening in Louisiana public elementary schools. *HortTechnology, 15*(3), 439-443.

Once weekly use of gardening and hands-on classroom activities helps improve science achievement test scores.

Let Kids Be the Gardeners

Bailey, L. H. (1904). A children's garden. *Cornell nature-study leaflets* (p. 379). Albany, NY: J.B. Lyon Company, Printers.

Hyun, E., & Marshall, D. J. (2003). Teachable moment-oriented curriculum practice in early childhood education. *Journal of Curriculum Studies, 35*(1), 111-127.

Hyun and Marshall offer a critique that education is not just about teaching—teachers need to be learners as well, letting the child take the lead.

James, J. J., & Bixler, R. D. (2008). Children's role in meaning making through their participation in an environmental education program. *The Journal of Environmental Education, 39*(4), 44-59.

James and Bixler place emphasis on choices and direct experiences as important to making meaning and learning.

Rahm, J. (2002). Emergent learning opportunities in an inner city youth gardening program. *Journal of Research in Science Teaching, 39*(2), 164-184.

In an informal, experiential youth gardening program, a learning community emerged from the garden environment through students' engagement in activities they deemed valuable, meaningful and authentic.

Wake, S. J. (2007). Children's gardens: Answering 'the Call of the Child'? *Built Environment, 33*(4), 441-453.

Kids need to be involved in the design of gardens in addition to being garden participants.

Build Self-Efficacy: Setting Kids Up for Success

Bandura, A. (1997). *Self-efficacy: The exercise of control.* New York: Freeman.

Bandura, A. (2000). Exercise of human agency through collective efficacy. *Current Directions in Psychological Science, 9*(3), 75-78.

Bandura examines collective efficacy and the ways in which it fosters groups' motivational commitment to their missions, resilience to adversity, and accomplishments.

Bandura, A., Barbaranelli, C., Caprera, G., & Pastorelli, C. (1996). Multifaceted impact of self-efficacy beliefs on academic functioning. *Child Development, 67*(3), 1206-1222.

Children's beliefs that they can do well in academic subjects depend not just on how well they actually do, but on other measures such as peer relationships, parent participation, and confidence that they can manage their own learning.

Bandura, A. (1994). Self-efficacy. In V. S. Ramachaudran (Ed.), *Encyclopedia of human behavior* (Vol. 4) (pp. 71-81). New York: Academic Press. (Reprinted in H. Friedman [Ed.], Encyclopedia of mental health. San Diego: Academic Press, 1998). Retrieved from https://web.stanford.edu/~kcarmel/CC_BehavChange_Course/readings/Bandura_Selfefficacy_1994.htm

Bandura describes the theory of self-efficacy.

Berk, L. E., & Winsler, A. (1995). *Scaffolding children's learning: Vygotsky and early childhood education. NAEYC research into practice series* (Vol. 7). Washington, DC: National Association for the Education of Young Children.

Berk and Winsler discuss developmental psychologist Lev Vygotsky and his formation of the concept of scaffolding.

Dewey, J. (1938). *Experience and education.* New York: Simon & Schuster.

Montessori, M. (2004). Nature in education. In Gutek, G. L. (Ed.), *The Montessori method. The origins of an educational innovation: Including an abridged and annotated edition of Maria Montessori's The Montessori method* (p. 145). Lanham, MD: Rowman & Littlefield Publishers, Inc.

Zimmerman, B. (2000). Self-efficacy: An essential motive to learn. *Contemporary Educational Psychology, 25,* 82-91.

Zimmerman finds that self-efficacy is a highly effective predictor of students' motivation and learning.

Zurek, A., Torquati, J., & Acar, I. (2014). Scaffolding as a tool for environmental education in early childhood. *International Journal of Early Childhood, 2*(1), 27.

Educators used scaffolding effectively in an environmental education program to support children in their understanding of outdoor experiences.

Cultivate a Sense of Wonder

Carson, R. (1956). *The sense of wonder* (p. 45). New York, NY: Harper & Row.

Carson makes a strong case for the importance of wonder and emotional connection to a child's education and later growth as an adult.

Davis, B., Rea, T., & Waite, S. (2006). The special nature of the outdoors: Its contribution to the education of children aged 3-11. *Australian Journal of Outdoor Education, 10*(2), 3.

Following E.O. Wilson, the authors suggest that biophilia may offer an explanation for why we learn well outdoors. The paper also elaborates on Kellert's typology of values associated with nature.

Dunlap, J., & Kellert, S. R. (Eds.). (2012). *Companions in wonder: Children and adults exploring nature together* (Vol. 8). Cambridge, MA: MIT Press.

This edited volume is an expansion of Rachel Carson's concepts and contains thirty essays on what a sense of wonder means and why it matters.

Engage the Senses

Cornell, J. (1998). *Sharing nature with children* (pp. 74-75). Nevada City, CA: DAWN Publications.

Cosco, N., & Moore, R. (2009). Sensory integration and contact with nature: Designing outdoor inclusive environments. *The NAMTA Journal, 34*(2), 158-176.

Cosco and Moore present research-based design guidelines for creating outdoor spaces that promote physical and mental health and development for children.

Louv, R. (2005). *Last child in the woods: Saving our children from Nature-Deficit Disorder* (p. 1). Chapel Hill, NC: Algonquin Books of Chapel Hill.

Louv provides a compelling and well-researched argument for the importance of, and need for, nature in children's lives.

Moore, R. (2007). *Plants for play* (p. 10). Berkeley, CA: MIG Communications

Pollan, M. (1991). *Second nature: A gardener's education* (p. 21). New York, NY: Dell Publishing.

Pollan explores the garden as a vital place to learn important lessons about our relationship with nature.

Build Learning Communities

Bouillion, L. M., & Gomez, L. M. (2001). Connecting school and community with science learning: Real world problems and school–community partnerships as contextual scaffolds. *Journal of Research in Science Teaching, 38*(8), 878-898.

Bouillion and Gomez explore a form of connected science that bridges community-based knowledge and school-based knowledge.

Finn, J. L., & Checkoway, B. (1998). Young people as competent community builders: A challenge to social work. *Social Work, 43*(4), 335-345

Finn and Checkoway present a pilot study that highlights six initiatives involving young people as community builders.

Hazzard, E. L., Moreno, E., Beall, D. L., & Zidenberg-Cherr, S. (2011). Best practices models for implementing, sustaining, and using instructional school gardens in California. *Journal of Nutrition Education and Behavior, 43*(5), 409-413.

Results from a study of exemplary school gardens in California found that having a committee that included administrators, teachers, parent and community volunteers, and garden coordinators who were committed to school gardens was the most important step to success.

hooks, b. (2010). *Teaching critical thinking: Practical wisdom.* New York, NY: Routledge.

hooks emphasizes the importance of teachers and students engaging in critical thinking and the creation of learning communities together.

Rogoff, B., Matusov, E., & White, C. (1996) Models of teaching and learning: Participation in a community of learners. In D. R. Olsen & N. Torrance (Eds.), *The handbook of education and human development* (pp. 388-414). Hoboken, NJ: John Wiley & Sons.

This book chapter discusses a theory of development where learning is cast as a community process of transformation and participation.

Smith, L. H. (2011). Piloting the use of teen mentors to promote a healthy diet and physical activity among children in Appalachia. *Journal for Specialists in Pediatric Nursing, 16*(1), 16-26.

Mentored children have greater positive health outcomes, including body mass index, efficacy, knowledge and attitudes, than those without mentors.

Tangen, D., & Fielding-Barnsley, R. (2007). Environmental education in a culturally diverse school. *Australian Journal of Environmental Education, 23*, 23.

ESL students who were part of an Australian school gardening program had positive gains in in-class learning through experiential learning in the garden. In addition, they experienced a feeling of belonging to their school community. The study also noted that teachers' commitment to the gardening program was vital to student success.

Thorp, L., & Townsend, C. (2001, December). Agricultural education in an elementary school: An ethnographic study of a school garden. In *Proceedings of the 28th Annual National Agricultural Education Research Conference in New Orleans*, LA, 347-360.

An exploration and case study of children's relationship to land and food.

Engage Kids in Meaningful Fitness

Dyment, J., & Bell, A. (2008). Grounds for movement: Green school grounds as sites for promoting physical activity. *Health Education Research, 23*(6), 952-62.

Green school grounds, which have a greater diversity of landscape and design features, can increase physical activity in children, complementing structured physical activities with opportunities for unstructured play and exploration.

Hermann, J., Parker, S., Brown, B., Siewe, Y., Denney, B., & Walker, S. (2006). After-school gardening improves children's reported vegetable intake and physical activity. *Journal of Nutrition Education and Behavior, 38*(3), 201-202.

Incorporating gardening is an effective way to improve vegetable intake and physical activity in an after-school setting.

Wells, N. M., Myers, B. M., & Henderson, C. R. (2014). School gardens and physical activity: A randomized controlled trial of low-income elementary schools. *Preventive Medicine, 69*, S27-S33.

A randomized study across multiple schools indicates that gardening may increase children's physical activity in several different ways.

Immerse Yourself in Nature

Carson, R. (1956). *The sense of wonder* (p. 95). New York, NY: Harper & Row.

Carson makes a strong case for the importance of wonder and emotional connection to a child's education and later growth as an adult.

Frumkin, H. (2001). Beyond toxicity: Human health and the natural environment. *American Journal of Preventive Medicine, 20*, 234-240.

Frumkin examines research on positive health effects that can arise from a variety of environmental exposures.

Hartig, T., Mitchell, R., de Vries, S., & Frumkin, H. (2014). Nature and health. *Annual Review of Public Health, 35*, 21.1-21.22.

This review examines research on the positive health impacts of nature, with a focus on aspects of the physical environment relevant to planning, design, and policy in urban settings.

Kaplan, R. & Kaplan, S. (1989). *The experience of nature: A psychological perspective* (p. 191). Cambridge: Cambridge University Press.

Kaplan and Kaplan provide an evidence-based analysis of the relationship between people and nature, particularly with respect to perceptions, preferences, and feelings.

Kaplan, S. (1995). The restorative benefits of nature: Toward an integrative framework. *Journal of Environmental Psychology, 15*(3), 169-82.

Kaplan describes Attention Restoration Theory and the restorative benefits of nature.

Pollan, M. (1991). *Second nature: A gardener's education* (p. 4). New York, NY: Dell Publishing.

Pollan explores the garden as a vital place to learn important lessons about our relationship with nature.

Taylor, A. F., Kuo, F. E., & Sullivan, W. C. (2001). Coping with ADD: The surprising connection to green play settings. *Environment and Behavior, 33*(1), 54-77.

Using Attention Restoration Theory, the authors propose that green environments are supportive for children with ADHD.

Wells, N. M., & Evans, G. W. (2003). Nearby nature: A buffer of life stress among rural children. *Environment and Behavior, 35*(3), 311-330.

In a rural setting, levels of nearby nature moderated the impact of stressful life events on the psychological well-being of children.

Make Connections to Home and Community

Armstrong, D. (2000). A survey of community gardens in upstate New York: Implications for health promotion and community development. *Health & Place, 6*(4), 319-327.

Research on twenty community garden programs found benefits that facilitate neighborhood development and health promotion.

Blair, D. (2009). The child in the garden: An evaluative review of the benefits of school gardening. *The Journal of Environmental Education, 40*(2), 15-38.

Blair reviews qualitative and quantitative evaluative literature on children's gardening, with various positive outcomes discussed.

Carney, P. A., Hamada, J. L., Rdesinski, R., Sprager, L., Nichols, K. R., Liu, B. Y., & Shannon, J. (2012). Impact of a community gardening project on vegetable intake, food security and family relationships: A community-based participatory research study. *Journal of Community Health, 37*(4), 874-881.

A community gardening program can reduce food insecurity, improve dietary intake and strengthen family relationships.

Israel, G. D., Beaulieu, L. J., & Hartless, G. H. (2001). The influence of family and community social capital on educational achievement. *Rural Sociology, 66*(1), 43-68.

Community and family engagement influences multiple child outcomes, including social skills, behavior, self-esteem, and academics.

Engage with Worms, Bees, Chickens and Other Animals

Basile, C., & White, C. (2000). Respecting living things: Environmental literacy for young children. *Early Childhood Education Journal, 28*(1), 57-61.

Children's behavior changed positively toward living things and each other during the course of an environmental literacy project that involved time outdoors.

Bratman, G. N., Hamilton, J. P., & Daily, G. C. (2012). The impacts of nature experience on human cognitive function and mental health. *Annals of the New York Academy of Sciences, 1249*(1), 118-136.

This paper provides an overview of the effects of nature experience on human cognitive function and mental health.

Esposito, L., McCune, S., Griffin, J. A., & Maholmes, V. (2011). Directions in human–animal interaction research: Child development, health, and therapeutic interventions. *Child Development Perspectives, 5*(3), 205-211.

The authors review research and key themes on how animal interaction affects children and promotes optimal development.

Frumkin, H. (2001). Beyond toxicity: Human health and the natural environment. *American Journal of Preventive Medicine, 20*(3), 234-240.

Frumkin examines research on positive health effects that can arise from a variety of environmental exposures.

Wilson, E. O. (1984). *Biophilia* (p. 2). Cambridge, MA: Harvard University Press.

Work *and* Play in the Garden

American Society for Microbiology. (2010, May 25). Can bacteria make you smarter?. *Science Daily*. Retrieved from www.sciencedaily.com/releases/2010/05/100524143416.htm

Exposure to specific bacteria in the environment, already believed to have antidepressant qualities, could potentially increase learning behavior as well.

Brown, S. L. (2009). *Play: How it shapes the brain, opens the imagination, and invigorates the soul.* New York, NY: Penguin.

Channick, R. (2010, March 24). NU study: Dirt's good for kids. *The Chicago Tribune*. Retrieved from http://articles.chicagotribune.com

This article describes research that found kids who had higher levels of exposure to infectious microbes as infants had lower levels of CRP (a predictive biomarker of cardiovascular heart disease and stroke) as young adults.

Frost, J., Wortham, S., & Reifel, R. (2008). *Play and child development.* Upper Saddle River, NJ: Pearson/Merrill Prentice Hall.

Ginsburg, K. R. (2007). The importance of play in promoting healthy child development and maintaining strong parent-child bonds. *Pediatrics, 119*(1), 182-191.

Play is essential to development because it contributes to the cognitive, physical, social, and emotional well-being of children.

Lowry, C. A., Hollis, J. H., de Vries, A., Pan, B., Brunet, L. R., ... & Lightman, S. L. (2007). Identification of an immune-responsive mesolimbocortical serotonergic system: Potential role in regulation of emotional behavior. *Neuroscience, 146*(2), 756-772.

The authors suggest that exposure to certain pathogens may positively impact anxiety, depression, and coping responses.

Platts-Mills, T. A., Erwin, E., Heymann, P., & Woodfolk, J. (2005). Is the hygiene hypothesis still a viable explanation for the increased prevalence of asthma? *Allergy, 60*(s79), 25-31.

This paper examines the usefulness of the hygiene hypothesis as an explanation for the increase in asthma in populations and outlines its limitations.

Ruebush, M. (2009). *Why dirt is good: 5 ways to make germs your friends*. Berkshire, UK: Kaplan Publishing.

Ruebush has written an accessible book for adults on the hygiene hypothesis.

Strachan, D. P. (2000). Family size, infection and atopy: The first decade of the 'hygiene hypothesis.' *Thorax, 55*(Suppl 1), S2.

Strachan examines the hygiene hypothesis in the context of a decade of research.

UN General Assembly. (1989). Convention on the Rights of the Child. *United Nations: Treaty Series*, 1577 (p. 3), Retrieved from www.refworld.org/docid/3ae6b38f0.html

Play is recognized as a human right by the United Nations.

Yazdanbakhsh, M., Kremsner, P. G., & Van Ree, R. (2002). Allergy, parasites, and the hygiene hypothesis. *Science, 296*(5567), 490-494.

The authors propose that bacterial, parasitic, and viral infections during early life may positively impact the immune system, and cite evidence based on worldwide research.

Utilize an Integrated Curriculum

Carver, G. W. (1910). Nature study and gardening for rural schools. *Tuskegee Normal and Industrial Institute Experiment Station Bulletin 18* (p. 5). Tuskagee, AL: Tuskagee Normal and Industrial Institute.

Drake, S. (2012). *Creating standards-based integrated curriculum: Common core edition (3rd edition)*. Thousand Oaks, CA: Corwin Press.

Integrated curricula and project-based learning can be aligned with Common Core and other academic standards.

Drake, S. M. & Reid, J. L. (2010). Integrated curriculum: Increasing relevance while maintaining accountability. *What works? Research into practice*. Toronto, ON: Ontario Ministry of Education. Retrieved from http://www.edu.gov.on.ca/eng/literacynumeracy/inspire/research/ww_Integrated_Curriculum.pdf

Integrated curricula and project-based learning are effective ways to teach students.

Krajcik, J., McNeil, K., & Reiser, B. (2007). Learning-goals-driven design model: Developing curriculum materials that align with national standards and incorporate project-based pedagogy. *Science Education, 92*(1), 1-32.

An integrated, project-based curriculum built on national science standards resulted in substantial and meaningful learning gains in students.

Leopold, A. (1991). The role of wildlife in a liberal education. In S. L. Flader & J. B. Callicott (Eds.), *The river of the mother of God and other essays by Aldo Leopold* (p. 302). Madison, WI: University of Wisconsin Press.

Cultivate a Connection to Food

Gatto, N., Ventura, E., Cook, L., Gyllenhammer, L., & Davis, J. (2012). LA Sprouts: A garden-based nutrition intervention pilot program influences motivation and preferences for fruits and vegetables in Latino youth. *Journal of the Academy of Nutrition and Dietetics, 112*(6), 913-920.

A cooking, nutrition, and gardening after-school program in a garden-based setting improved attitudes and preferences for fruits and vegetables in Latino youth.

Heim, S., Bauer, K. W., Stang, J., & Ireland, M. (2011). Can a community-based intervention improve the home food environment? Parental perspectives of the influence of the delicious and nutritious garden. *Journal of Nutrition Education and Behavior, 43*(2), 130-134.

Pre-post surveys of parents whose 4th-6th grade children participated in a summer camp gardening program found an increase in the frequency children asked for fruits and vegetables at home, as well as an increase in home availability of fruits and vegetables, and parental encouragement of fruits and vegetables consumption.

Hermann, J. R., Parker, S. P., Brown, B. J., Siewe, Y. J., Denney, B. A., & Walker, S. J. (2006). After-school gardening improves children's reported vegetable intake and physical activity. *Journal of Nutrition Education and Behavior, 38*(3), 201-202.

Incorporating gardening is an effective way to improve vegetable intake and physical activity in an after-school setting.

Kimmerer, R. W. (2013). *Braiding sweetgrass: Indigenous wisdom, scientific knowledge, and the teachings of plants* (p. 129). Minneapolis, MN: Milkweed Editions.

McAleese, J. D., & Rankin, L. L. (2007). Garden-based nutrition education affects fruit and vegetable consumption in sixth-grade adolescents. *Journal of the American Dietetic Association, 107*(4), 662-665.

Adolescents who participated in a garden-based nutrition intervention increased their servings of fruits and vegetables more than students in two other groups.

Ratcliffe, M., Merrigan, K., Rogers, B., & Goldberg, J. (2011). The effects of school garden experiences on middle school-aged students' knowledge, attitudes, and behaviors associated with vegetable consumption. *Health Promotion Practice, 12*(1), 36-43.

School gardening may affect children's vegetable consumption, including improved recognition of, attitudes toward, preferences for, and willingness to taste vegetables.

Robinson-O'Brien, R., Story, M., & Heim, S. (2009). Impact of garden-based youth nutrition intervention programs: A review. *Journal of the American Dietetic Association, 109*(2), 273-280.

Garden-based nutrition interventions may have the potential to promote increased fruit and vegetable intake among youth and increase willingness to taste fruits and vegetables among younger children.

Cultivate a Sense of Place

Derr, V. (2002). Children's sense of place in Northern New Mexico. *Journal of Environmental Psychology, 22*(1-2), 125-37.

Derr demonstrates the important role that extended family and direct experience play in shaping children's sense of place and understanding of nature.

Gesler, W. (1992). Therapeutic landscapes: Medical issues in light of new cultural geography. *Social Science and Medicine, 34*(7), 735-46.

Gesler explores why certain places or situations are perceived to be therapeutic, using themes and illustrations from work in cultural geography and the literature of the social science of health care.

Lengen, C., & Kistemann, T. (2012). Sense of place and place identity: Review of neuroscientific evidence. *Health & Place, 18*(5), 1162-71.

Lengen and Kistemann review the evidence for the biological basis of sense of place.

Measham, T. (2007). Primal landscapes: Insights for education from empirical research on ways of learning about environments. *International Research on Geographical and Environmental Education, 16*(4), 339-50.

Measham discusses "primal landscapes" as a way of conceptualizing interactions between children and their environments. The author draws on empirical research conducted in human geography and emphasizes the importance of involving elders and family in environmental education.

Nabhan, G., & Trimble, S. (1994). *The geography of childhood* (p. xiii). Boston, MA: Beacon Press.

Pyle, R. M. (2011). *The thunder tree: Lessons from an urban wildland* (pp. 2-3). Corvallis, OR: Oregon State University Press.

Sobel, D. (1998). *Mapmaking with children: Sense of place education for the elementary years.* Portsmouth, NH: Heinemann.

Mapmaking with Children introduces children to mapmaking through hands-on neighborhood/ backyard projects, while emphasizing the importance of a sense of place in children's lives.

Epilogue: Growing Hope

Kiss the Ground. (2018, September 27). 5 Ways to Make your Garden Regenerative [Video file]. https://www.youtube.com/watch?v=kK6NrUmrV4A

Maathai, W. M. (2006) *Unbowed: A memoir* (p. 138). New York, NY: Anchor Books.

nicopirrus. (2009, January 12). Terra Madre 2008 — Sam Levin opening speech. Pt. 2 [Video file]. https://www.youtube.com/watch?v=ph1OVHbAKsQ

Sobel, D. (1996). *Beyond ecophobia: Reclaiming the heart in nature education* (p.32). Great Barrington, MA: The Orion Society.

About the Team

Nathan Kennard Larson has worked in the fields of nature-, farm-, and garden-based education since the dawn of the 21st century. Over the past two decades, he has enjoyed and felt deeply grateful for many opportunities to work with students, educators, colleagues, and community partners to establish and grow vibrant garden-based education programs and networks. He currently leads the Cultivate Health Initiative, a joint public health project of Rooted and the Environmental Design Lab at UW-Madison to grow and sustain the school garden network and movement in Wisconsin. He also serves on the board

of the National School Garden Network and on his local school district's Wellness Advisory Council. Nathan lives and tends a garden with his wife and two children in Madison, Wisconsin.

Becky Hiller is a local Madison artist who enjoys creating art with a variety of media, gardening veggies and flowers, and working with young people. She worked closely with Nathan Kennard Larson to illustrate this book, and bring to life the vibrant energy of Rooted's youth gardens.

Alex Wells is the Managing Director of the Environmental Design Lab, whose mission is healthy places for everyone. She manages the research, implementation, and evaluation of projects related to kids' health and well-being, neighborhood placemaking, outdoor learning, and garden-based education.

Samuel Dennis, Jr. is Professor of Landscape Architecture at UW-Madison and the Research Director of the Environmental Design Lab. His work focuses on understanding and designing outdoor environments that support health and well-being with an emphasis on young people. He uses participatory methods to engage people in community planning, design, and placemaking.

Whitney Cohen is the Education Director at Life Lab and a lecturer at UC Santa Cruz. She is a teacher, trainer, and author with tremendous commitment to, and expertise in, place-based education, student-led inquiry, strategies for engaging a diverse student population, school gardens, and the intersection between environmental education and the public school system.

Mary Kay Warner is the owner of Sandhill Studio LLC. She was the art director on *Teaching in Nature's Classroom*.

Lightning Source UK Ltd.
Milton Keynes UK
UKHW050348011122
411424UK00003B/191